EXPLORING THE STATES

Oregon

THE BEAVER STATE

by Emily Rose Oachs

BELLWETHER MEDIA • MINNEAPOLIS, MN

Note to Librarians, Teachers, and Parents:

Blastoff! Readers are carefully developed by literacy experts and combine standards-based content with developmentally appropriate text.

Level 1 provides the most support through repetition of high-frequency words, light text, predictable sentence patterns, and strong visual support.

Level 2 offers early readers a bit more challenge through varied simple sentences, increased text load, and less repetition of high-frequency words.

Level 3 advances early-fluent readers toward fluency through increased text and concept load, less reliance on visuals, longer sentences, and more literary language.

Level 4 builds reading stamina by providing more text per page, increased use of punctuation, greater variation in sentence patterns, and increasingly challenging vocabulary.

Level 5 encourages children to move from "learning to read" to "reading to learn" by providing even more text, varied writing styles, and less familiar topics.

Whichever book is right for your reader, Blastoff! Readers are the perfect books to build confidence and encourage a love of reading that will last a lifetime!

This edition first published in 2014 by Bellwether Media, Inc.

No part of this publication may be reproduced in whole or in part without written permission of the publisher. For information regarding permission, write to Bellwether Media, Inc., Attention: Permissions Department, 5357 Penn Avenue South, Minneapolis, MN 55419.

Library of Congress Cataloging-in-Publication Data

Oachs, Emily Rose.
Oregon / by Emily Rose Oachs.
    pages cm. – (Blastoff! readers. Exploring the states)
Includes bibliographical references and index.
Summary: "Developed by literacy experts for students in grades three through seven, this book introduces young readers to the geography and culture of Oregon"–Provided by publisher.
ISBN 978-1-62617-036-0 (hardcover : alk. paper)
1. Oregon–Juvenile literature. I. Title.
F876.3.O24 2014
979.5–dc23
                                                                    2013005583

Printed in the United States of America, North Mankato, MN.

Table of Contents

Where Is Oregon?

Oregon lies along the West Coast of the United States. The state has about 296 miles (476 kilometers) of shoreline. Salem, the capital city, sits beside the Willamette River in Oregon's northwestern corner.

Washington borders Oregon to the north. The Columbia River forms much of this boundary. The Snake River creates part of Oregon's eastern border. Across the river is Idaho. Nevada and California are Oregon's southern neighbors. To the west is the Pacific Ocean.

Pacific
Ocean

Washington

Columbia River

● Portland

★ **Salem**

Willamette River

Snake River

● Eugene

Oregon

Idaho

California **Nevada**

Did you know?

The Snake River carved out
Hells Canyon between Oregon
and Idaho. Hells Canyon plunges
7,900 feet (2,408 meters). That is
deeper than the Grand Canyon!

N
W   E
S

About 125 groups of **Native** Americans lived in Oregon when Europeans first arrived. In 1843, about 900 **pioneers** traveled the Oregon Trail to Oregon country. Some settled on Native American land. The Native Americans and pioneers sometimes fought. Eventually, the U.S. government moved most of Oregon's Native Americans to **reservations**.

Did you know?

The Oregon Trail extended more than 2,000 miles (3,219 kilometers) from Missouri to Oregon. In nineteen years, 50,000 people traveled the route. The ruts left by wagon wheels can still be seen in some places.

Oregon Trail

Oregon Timeline!

1792: American fur trader Robert Gray explores the Columbia River.

1805: Meriwether Lewis and William Clark reach Oregon's coast while exploring the West.

1843: The first group of settlers to use the Oregon Trail arrives in Oregon.

1844: A new law makes slavery illegal. It demands that African Americans leave Oregon country.

1850: The Oregon Donation Land Law gives free land to settlers.

1859: Oregon becomes the thirty-third state.

1877: Chief Joseph flees from U.S. troops with more than 400 Native Americans.

1883: All of Oregon's Native American tribes have been sent to reservations.

1912: Oregon is among the first states to give women the right to vote.

1938: Construction of the Bonneville Dam is completed. This is a major dam on the Columbia River.

Lewis and Clark

Chief Joseph

Bonneville Dam construction

The Land

Mount Hood

Oregon's Climate
average °F

spring
Low: 39°
High: 60°

summer
Low: 51°
High: 78°

fall
Low: 41°
High: 63°

winter
Low: 30°
High: 45°

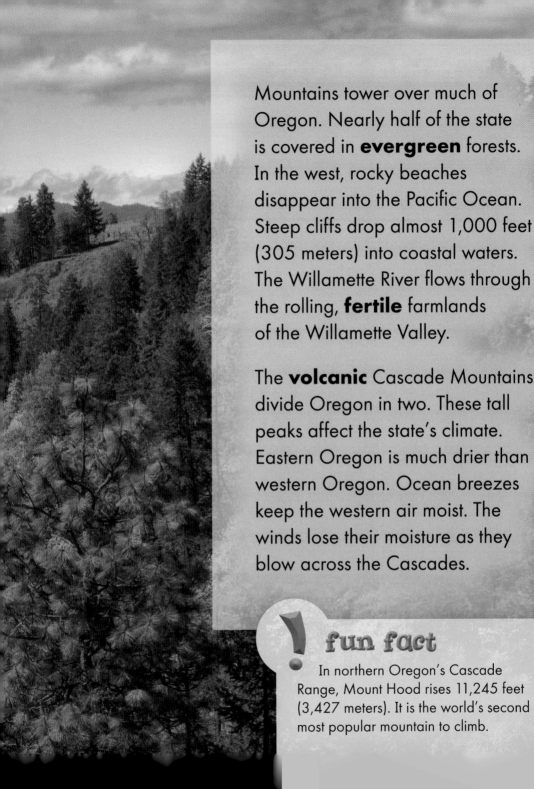

Mountains tower over much of Oregon. Nearly half of the state is covered in **evergreen** forests. In the west, rocky beaches disappear into the Pacific Ocean. Steep cliffs drop almost 1,000 feet (305 meters) into coastal waters. The Willamette River flows through the rolling, **fertile** farmlands of the Willamette Valley.

The **volcanic** Cascade Mountains divide Oregon in two. These tall peaks affect the state's climate. Eastern Oregon is much drier than western Oregon. Ocean breezes keep the western air moist. The winds lose their moisture as they blow across the Cascades.

fun fact

In northern Oregon's Cascade Range, Mount Hood rises 11,245 feet (3,427 meters). It is the world's second most popular mountain to climb.

Columbia River

The Columbia River flows 1,240 miles (1,996 kilometers). It winds through Canada, Washington, and Oregon on its way to the Pacific. For 300 miles (483 kilometers), it marks the boundary between Washington and Oregon.

For thousands of years, Native Americans lived along the banks of the Columbia River. Each year, they gathered near what is now the City of The Dalles. They traded and fished for salmon along the rocky riverbanks. In the 1800s, the Oregon Trail's land route ended at The Dalles. From there, some pioneers rafted down the Columbia to the Willamette Valley. Today, many **dams** cross the Columbia River. They provide **hydroelectricity** for the area.

Bonneville Dam

Columbia River Gorge

Did you know?
The Bonneville Dam was built on the Columbia River just east of Portland. It produces enough power to provide energy to hundreds of thousands of homes.

Wildlife

All kinds of wildlife fill the lands and waters of Oregon. Mountain goats step lightly across Oregon's rugged mountaintops. Canada lynx prowl for prey on top of deep mountain snow. Foxes build their dens in the **foothills** of the mountains. West of the Cascades, black bears forage for food. In eastern Oregon, pronghorns are easy to spot with their long, curved horns. Prickly porcupines live in the pine forests.

Furry minks swim and hunt in rivers. Beavers build their dams in ponds and streams. Oregon's coastal waters are home to sea lions, seals, and sea otters. There they hunt for cod and other ocean prey.

sea otter

fox

Canada lynx

Did you know?

Every year, thousands of salmon leave the ocean to lay their eggs in Oregon's rivers. The salmon leap over low waterfalls that stand in their way!

salmon

The Cascade Mountains are home to some of Oregon's most beautiful landmarks. Mount Hood National Forest spreads over 1,700 square miles (4,403 square kilometers) of mountains and forests. Crater Lake fills a **caldera** that was once a volcano peak. It is known for its clear blue water and great depth.

Crater Lake

Heceta Head Lighthouse

Perched on the Pacific coast, Heceta Head Lighthouse draws photographers from all over the state. The Favell Museum in Klamath Falls is dedicated to Native American art. It owns more than 100,000 **artifacts**, including arrowheads and beadwork.

Portland

Portland is Oregon's largest city. It sits in the Willamette Valley in northwestern Oregon. Portland was built on the Willamette River, near where it joins with the Columbia. People call it the "City of Roses." Its mild weather is perfect for growing these flowers.

Portland is known for its music scene. People go out to the city's many **venues** to watch local musicians perform. Portlanders also like to support local farms. Many restaurants buy fresh ingredients directly from nearby farms. In their free time, Portlanders stroll or bike through the public parks and gardens that dot the city.

Working

Did you know?

An Oregon law says that drivers cannot pump their own gas. Workers at gas stations do it for them!

Many Oregonians have **service jobs**. They serve the state's **tourists** at hotels, restaurants, and stores. The Willamette Valley has some of Oregon's most fertile farmland. Oregon farmers grow flowers and other plants for gardens. The state is also a leading producer of raspberries and peppermint.

Oregon's forests provide plenty of lumber. The trees are cut down to make wood and paper products for the nation. Factories around Portland produce electronics, metals, and machinery. Miners dig for sand and gravel throughout the state.

Where People Work in Oregon

manufacturing
9%

services
74%

farming and
natural resources
4%

government
13%

Playing

Oregon's many parks allow for a lot of outdoor activities. People camp and hike in the mountains and grasslands. Bird-watchers grab their binoculars to watch **migrating** birds pass over Oregon. Fishers head to streams and rivers to catch steelhead and other trout. Some even dangle lines from their kayaks.

Oregonians ski and snowboard year-round at the Timberline Lodge in the Mount Hood National Forest. Some 10,000 people try to climb Mount Hood each year. **Windsurfing** competitions are held at the Columbia River Gorge near the Hood River. This area is known as the Windsurfing Capital of the World.

windsurfing

Oregon Hazelnut Trail Mix

Ingredients:

6 cups Kix cereal

1 1/2 cups coarsely chopped or whole roasted hazelnuts

1 cup golden raisins

1 cup banana chips

1 small package non-instant vanilla pudding

1/2 cup honey

1/2 cup peanut butter

Directions:

1. Mix cereal, nuts, raisins, and banana chips together.

2. In saucepan, combine vanilla pudding and honey. Bring to a boil and boil 30 seconds.

3. Remove from heat. Stir in peanut butter. Mix well.

4. Pour over cereal mixture and mix until coated. Cool on cookie sheet.

hazelnuts

Did you know?
Hazelnuts are sweet nuts from hazel trees. Almost all of the hazelnuts grown in the United States are from the Willamette Valley.

seafood
lasagna

Many Oregonians prepare dishes using fresh ingredients from farmers' markets. Summers bring heaps of colorful berries. People like to bake sweet **marionberries** into pies. The state is also known for its many types of mushrooms. Cooks toss salads with fresh mushrooms, lettuce, and hazelnuts.

Oregon's coastal waters provide fresh seafood. Dungeness crab is the special ingredient in a creamy soup. Chefs dice up fresh seafood to make shrimp, salmon, and crab cakes. Sometimes Oregonians bake the day's catch with noodles and cheese to make seafood lasagna.

Festivals

In February, the Portland International Film Festival draws over 35,000 people. More than 100 films **premiere** at this event. The Oregon Shakespeare Festival runs from February through November in Ashland. During summer, people can watch Shakespeare's plays outdoors.

Oregonians gather for Portland's Rose Festival in June. Everyone wants to see the Grand Floral Parade. Marching bands and flowery floats wind through Portland's streets. In August, people head to Salem for the Oregon State Fair. The Pendleton Round-Up is a four-day **rodeo** in September. Oregonians come from all over to watch bull riding and enjoy the carnival.

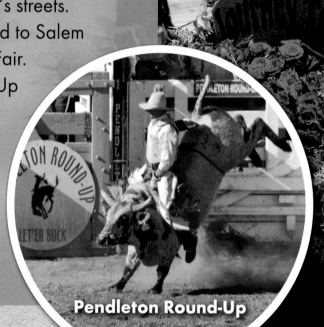

Pendleton Round-Up

Rose Festival
Grand Floral Parade

fun fact

In 1950, Evelyn and Paul Trent spotted an Unidentified Flying Object near their home outside McMinnville. Each year, the city holds a UFO Festival to honor the sighting.

Bicycling

Oregonians are famous for bicycling, both for fun and transportation. Portland, Eugene, and Salem are all known as some of the nation's best biking cities. Shops and stores set aside plenty of space for bicycle parking. Kidical Mass and other groups organize fun bike rides for kids and their families.

Did you know?
Portland is often called the most bike-friendly city in the country. About 8 out of every 100 people pedal to work each day.

Hundreds of miles of bike paths wind through Oregon. **Bike boulevards** snake through the cities. These make it easier for people to pedal to work instead of driving. Oregonians know that their state's natural beauty is precious. Biking is an Earth-friendly way to enjoy it.

Fast Facts About Oregon

STATE OF OREGON

1859

Oregon's Flag

Oregon's navy blue flag has designs on both sides. The front features a golden shield and the year of statehood. The thirty-three stars around the shield show that Oregon was the thirty-third state. Inside the shield are items important to Oregon's history, including a covered wagon and a forest. The back of the flag features a golden beaver.

State Flower
Oregon grape

State Nickname:	Beaver State
State Motto:	"She Flies With Her Own Wings"
Year of Statehood:	1859
Capital City:	Salem
Other Major Cities:	Portland, Eugene
Population:	3,831,074 (2010)
Area:	97,048 square miles (251,353 square kilometers); Oregon is the 10th largest state.
Major Industries:	farming, manufacturing, services, tourism
Natural Resources:	lumber, water, soil, sand, gravel
State Government:	60 representatives; 30 senators
Federal Government:	5 representatives; 2 senators
Electoral Votes:	7

State Animal
beaver

State Bird
western meadowlark

Glossary

artifacts—items made long ago by humans; artifacts tell people today about people from the past.

bike boulevards—streets that do not have a lot of traffic and are used mostly by bicyclists and pedestrians

caldera—a crater created when a volcanic peak collapses

dams—structures that block the flow of water in rivers

evergreen—a tree that stays green and does not lose its leaves in winter; most evergreen trees in Oregon are pine trees.

fertile—able to support growth

foothills—hills at the base of a mountain

hydroelectricity—power produced by the force of running water

marionberries—sweet berries similar to blackberries

migrating—traveling from one place to another, often with the seasons

native—originally from a specific place

pioneers—people who are among the first to explore or settle in an area

premiere—to show for the first time

reservations—areas of land the government has set aside for Native Americans

rodeo—an event where people compete in tasks such as bull riding and calf roping; cowboys once completed these tasks as part of their daily work.

service jobs—jobs that perform tasks for people or businesses

tourists—people who travel to visit another place

venues—places that hold events such as concerts

volcanic—relating to volcanoes; volcanoes are holes in the earth that spew hot, melted rock called lava.

windsurfing—a sport in which people ride over water on a board with a sail

To Learn More

AT THE LIBRARY

Aronin, Miriam. *How Many People Traveled the Oregon Trail? And Other Questions About the Trail West*. Minneapolis, Minn.: Lerner Publishing Group, 2012.

Biskup, Agnieszka. *Thunder Rolling Down the Mountain: The Story of Chief Joseph and the Nez Perce*. Mankato, Minn.: Capstone Press, 2011.

Cleary, Beverly. *Ramona Quimby, Age 8*. New York, N.Y.: HarperCollins, 2013.

ON THE WEB

Learning more about Oregon is as easy as 1, 2, 3.

1. Go to www.factsurfer.com.

2. Enter "Oregon" into the search box.

3. Click the "Surf" button and you will see a list of related Web sites.

With factsurfer.com, finding more information is just a click away.

Index